THOMAS NAST'S
CHRISTMAS DRAWINGS
for the Human Race

THOMAS NAST'S
CHRISTMAS DRAWINGS
for the Human Race

WITH INTRODUCTION AND EPILOGUE BY

THOMAS NAST ST. HILL

HARPER & ROW, PUBLISHERS

NEW YORK, EVANSTON, SAN FRANCISCO,

LONDON

To the
memory of my grandparents
Thomas Nast and Sarah Edwards Nast

Contents

THOMAS NAST'S
CHRISTMAS DRAWINGS
for the Human Race

Introduction

Thomas Nast, America's foremost political cartoonist and the creator of the image of Santa Claus as we recognize him today, was born in 1840 in the military barracks in Landau, Bavaria, where his father was a musician in the Ninth Regiment Bavarian Band. The elder Nast, while not a disturber, was a man of liberal ideas, and, in view of the political turmoil then prevalent in Germany, his friendly commandant suggested that America might be a better place for a man so fond of free speech. So it was that the six-year-old Thomas and his mother and older sister departed for the United States in 1846 and settled in New York. Nast senior followed four years later after serving out his enlistment. Upon his arrival in New York he found employment in the orchestra of Burton's Theatre in Chambers Street and became a member of the Philharmonic Society.

Young as he was when leaving his native land, Thomas Nast brought with him memories that were to influence his career as an artist. One was his love of the German celebration of Christmas, with stockings hung by the chimney for the Christmas Eve visit of Pelz-Nicol. And he was never to forget the religious bigotry that he had witnessed in the land of his birth. The Nast family were Protestants and young Thomas had been confused by the conflicting views of Catholics and Protestants and their intolerance of one another's beliefs.

Following the arrival of the family in New York, Thomas and his older sister were entered in one of the city's public schools. The young German boy was handicapped by not being able to speak a word of English. Furthermore, it soon became apparent that he was no scholar. His only interest was in drawing and after six years of schooling it was decided that it would be best to allow him to pursue his obsession by transferring to art school. Here he proved an apt pupil with real artistic ability, but the income of the father musician was insufficient to keep the budding artist in a private academy. Consequently, at age fifteen, Thomas Nast's formal education was abruptly ended, and he went out into the world to earn his living. Surprisingly, he was offered a job following his first interview.

Appearing in the office of *Leslie's*, an illustrated news magazine published in New York, the short, roly-poly German boy was ushered into the presence of Frank Leslie, to whom he showed some of his drawings and explained that he would like to draw for the magazine. Seeking to impress the aspiring fifteen-year-old with the absurdity of his request, Leslie gave him an assignment. It was to go down to the

Nast's Caricature of His First
Interview with Frank Leslie.

Christopher Street ferry house in lower Manhattan during the rush hour and draw a
picture of the crowd boarding the ferry at the last call of "All Aboard!" To the publisher's great surprise, the young artist returned with a very commendable picture
that won him a job as illustrator with *Leslie's* at four dollars a week. For several years
thereafter Nast's drawings appeared in the magazine, and it was during this time that
he drew his first cartoons attacking civic dishonesty.

It was fortunate that Thomas Nast went to work when he did, for in 1858 his
father died and the artist, then eighteen, was obliged to contribute to the support of
his mother. Not long after, *Leslie's* was obliged to cut salaries because of financial
problems, and young Nast left the magazine and found employment in the art studio
of a friend. While there he made his first drawing for *Harper's Weekly*, and in 1859
a page of his pictures depicting the police scandal in New York City was accepted
by the magazine.

During these years the maturing young artist met and fell in love with Sarah Edwards, a cultured and charming young lady of English parentage, who would later
become his wife. Sally Edwards was blessed with a background and education such
as Thomas Nast had not been privileged to enjoy. Although his earnings had in-
creased to twenty dollars a week, Nast was hardly in a position to ask Miss Edwards'
hand in marriage. Accordingly, when an offer came to join the staff of the *New York
Illustrated News*, at twice his current salary, he jumped at it.

Next came an opportunity to go abroad for the *News* and send back pictures of

2

Thomas Nast at Nineteen.

the Heenan-Sayers heavyweight championship fight in England. Nast accepted the assignment, hoping that by so doing he could acquire the necessary nest egg on which to get married.

In February, 1860, the artist, not yet twenty years old, sailed for England, very much in love, as his letters home revealed, but not quite sure that his Sally would be waiting for him when he returned.

While in England, young Nast learned of Giuseppe Garibaldi's return from exile in South America to liberate his native Italy from Austrian domination. Garibaldi, "The Liberator," was the type of leader that appealed to the crusading spirit of Thomas Nast and, upon completion of his prizefight assignment, he decided to join Garibaldi's campaign as a war correspondent. But lack of funds presented a problem, as the *News*, not having the cash with which to pay the artist, had sent him its note for one hundred dollars. Fortunately Francis Heenan, the newly crowned heavyweight champion, came to his rescue. "The Benicia Boy," as he was called, took pity on his young friend and paid him in cash for the note, saying that if the *News* did not pay him off when he returned to New York he would knock their "damn Dutch heads off!"

Thomas Nast's assignment in England had not proven profitable in spite of Heenan's help, so when the *London Illustrated News* joined the *New York Illustrated News* in offering to send him to Italy to cover Garibaldi's expedition, the impecunious young artist, still hoping to acquire that nest egg, readily accepted, even though it would mean prolonging his absence from his beloved Sally. The artist served throughout the campaign and sailed for home following the successful completion of Garibaldi's mission. However, Thomas Nast was no better off financially when he returned to the United States after a year's absence than he had been when he left England six months earlier to join Garibaldi. But, most important, he found Sarah Edwards waiting for him and although he arrived home with only a dollar and a half in his pocket, he was not deterred from pressing his suit for her hand. Following his return, he again went to work for the *News* and finally prevailed upon Sally's parents to consent to their marriage, which took place on September 26, 1861, the day before Thomas Nast's twenty-first birthday. The bride was twenty.

When the Civil War broke out in April of 1861, Thomas Nast had considered enlisting, but those who knew of his talents convinced him that he could better serve his country with his pencil than with a sword. Thus it was that early in 1862 the young bridegroom, who had recently joined the staff of *Harper's Weekly*, was sent to the front as artist on the scene for that magazine. He was attracting nationwide attention with his Civil War drawings at the time Professor Clement Clarke Moore

Portrait of Clement Clarke Moore by Daniel Huntington, 1850.

finally got around to writing down his "Visit from St. Nicholas" poem, in March, 1862.

Dr. Moore had been a professor of Biblical Languages at New York's General Theological Seminary forty years earlier, when, snatching moments between classes, he had composed and memorized his poem as a Christmas Eve surprise for his six small children. Unlike his more serious literary contributions, this composition was not intended for posterity—in fact, he hadn't even bothered to write it down.

It was rather a rollicking poem, he thought, and if it merely brought a giggle from Charlie, a chuckle from Clement, and a knowing wink from Margaret, who was seven and knew everything, the professor would be more than satisfied.

So it happened, then, that after Christmas Eve supper, when the children were gathered about the fireplace all eager to learn what the professor had in store for them, he slowly began:

> " 'Twas the night before Christmas, when all through the house
> Not a creature was stirring, not even a mouse."

But if the professor's wife, Eliza, had not recorded the poem in the family album, the story of St. Nicholas' historic visit to the Moore household on that Christmas Eve of 1822 might never have been heard of again. There it was spotted by a friend of the family and passed along to the Troy, New York, *Sentinel*, where it made its first public appearance a year later. Thereafter, the poem appeared in print a few more times before 1862, when the elderly gentleman, then eighty-two years old, was prevailed upon by the New-York Historical Society to write the poem down in his own hand.

The young artist must have seen the poem soon after, for in that year's Christmas issue of *Harper's Weekly* appeared Nast's drawing of Santa Claus, with sleigh and reindeer, much as Moore had described him. But Thomas Nast could not forget Pelz-Nicol, the German counterpart of St. Nicholas, that he had known as a boy in his native Bavaria. Accordingly, the figure that appeared in his drawing "Santa Claus in Camp" was a combination of Moore's St. Nicholas and Germany's gnome-like Pelz-Nicol.

Nast's Christmas drawing marks the first appearance of Santa Claus as we know him today. Prior to this time, Santa had passed through a series of transformations, beginning with Asia Minor's very sedate Bishop of Myra in the fourth century, until he arrived in America as Sancte Klaas, a diminutive Dutch figure in short jacket and pantaloons, who personified the gift bringer in early nineteenth-century New Amsterdam.

So it may be said that Clement Moore, the learned American professor, and

The Original St. Nicholas.

Visit from St. Nicholas, "a diminutive Dutchman
in short jacket and pantaloons."

Thomas Nast, the young German-born artist, gave the world a new image of St. Nicholas and one that would live in the hearts of children for generations to come. But had Thomas Nast not brought Moore's "jolly old elf" to life in his drawings, the St. Nicholas described in Moore's poem might never have survived.

There was a poignant note in Santa Claus' wartime appearance in America, coming as it did when families from all parts of the country were separated. Nast, who had visited the battlefields, was sending back to *Harper's* sketches of grim scenes that he had witnessed, but he hoped in this drawing to cheer both the soldiers at the front and their loved ones at home. There were those who felt that in this picture Thomas Nast had done a disservice to Santa Claus in appropriating him for the Northern

Christmas in Camp.

cause, so evident in the United States flag and Santa in his star-spangled jacket and striped trousers. But the artist was one of the Union's staunchest supporters and everything he drew reflected his strong convictions.

While most of Nast's Civil War drawings were designed to arouse patriotic fervor on behalf of the Union cause, it was his semi-allegorical drawings that captured the imagination of the country. In the same issue in which his first Santa Claus picture appeared was a double-page spread entitled "Christmas Eve." It was a decorative combination of several drawings in the sentimental style so popular at the time. Wherever *Harper's Weekly* went, this picture touched a responsive chord. It was a time when almost every household knew the loneliness that comes with the separation of loved ones at Christmastime. Letters from every corner of the Union poured into *Harper's* with messages of thanks for that inspired picture.

A colonel wrote to tell how he had received his copy of the magazine and had unfolded it by the light of his campfire. He was so touched by Nast's drawing that tears had fallen on the page. "It was only a picture," he wrote, "but I couldn't help it."

Equally nostalgic is a second drawing that followed a year later entitled "Christmas Furlough," another composite picture in which the returning soldier is being welcomed home by his family. In both of these drawings the detail is remarkable, a characteristic that was to typify all of the artist's later work. Even in the small sketches that surround the main picture, each face is clearly delineated, as can be seen with the aid of a magnifying glass, all the more unusual when it is realized that the illustration was printed from a wood engraving. In wood engraving, the picture was first drawn in reverse in pencil on a block of soft wood. The spaces between the lines of the drawing were then gouged out or cut away with sharp instruments, leaving only the raised lines to be reproduced, just as type, when inked, prints the letters on the page.

Thomas Nast's emblematic cartoons in *Harper's* during the war so stirred the hearts of Northerners that President Lincoln referred to him as the Union's best recruiting sergeant. And at the close of the war, General Grant was to say that Thomas Nast had done as much as any one man to preserve the Union and bring the war to an end, a remarkable tribute to the young German-born artist.

Nast's relationship with *Harper's* was firmly established during the war years, and in the twenty years to follow the magazine and the artist would become champions of honesty in government and bulwarks of Republicanism.

In 1870 Nast launched an attack on the corrupt Tweed Ring of New York City in the pages of *Harper's Weekly*. While his campaign against "Boss" Tweed and his infamous Ring is familiar to students of American history, it is less well known that in

Christmas Eve.

Christmas Furlough.

1871 the artist refused a bribe of half a million dollars to call off his attacks and go abroad to study art. Tweed did not so much mind what the papers printed about him, he said, because most of his constituents couldn't read, but they could see "them damn pictures."

Failing in its attempt to bribe Nast, the Ring next threatened *Harper's* by throwing out all of the publisher's texts from the city schools and ordering the Tweed-controlled Board of Education to reject all future Harper & Brothers bids for school books. The Harpers' board of directors almost capitulated, but Nast's loyal friend, Fletcher Harper, stood by him and the fight went on. Nast continued his campaign against the Ring despite threats against his life, vowing that he would see them all in jail before he stopped. When suspicious-looking characters were observed loitering about his home in upper Manhattan and the friendly police captain in the neighborhood was suddenly transferred to another precinct, Nast decided that it was time to move his family out of the city to better ensure their safety. It was at this time that he bought Villa Fontana in suburban Morristown, New Jersey, which was to be the Nast home for the next thirty years.

Thomas Nast's cartoon, "The Tammany Tiger Loose," that appeared as a double-page spread in *Harper's* just before the fall elections in 1871, is considered one of the most powerful cartoons of all time and was principally responsible for the defeat of the Tweed Ring at the polls a few days later. It was printed from a wood engraving and all of Tweed's gang are clearly identifiable.

After being prosecuted for having looted the city of over thirty million dollars in the course of thirty months (a plasterer was paid almost three million dollars for nine months' work on the new City Hall), members of the Ring were jailed but Tweed himself managed to escape to Europe. There he was captured and returned to the United States. Ironically, Tweed was apprehended in Spain on a charge of kidnapping, this being one crime of which he had never been guilty. Authorities in this country, at a loss to understand the charge, later learned that Tweed had been recognized from a Nast cartoon that showed Tweed in prison garb with two little ragamuffins in tow. This was a cartoon that the artist had drawn some years earlier to illustrate Tweed's expressed willingness, when seeking the governorship of New York State, to bring all manner of lesser thieves to justice.

When Tweed died in New York City's Ludlow Street jail in 1878, every one of Nast's cartoons attacking him were found among his effects.

Thomas Nast's part in overthrowing the Tweed Ring added to the nationwide prominence he had gained during the war. He had become a political power, every Presidential candidate that he supported having been elected. Even General Grant,

The Tammany Tiger Loose. "What are you going to do about it?"

upon assuming the Presidency, attributed his election to the "sword of Sheridan and the pencil of Thomas Nast."

The symbols that Nast originated during this period were to far outlive their creator. Between 1870 and 1874 the Republican Elephant and the Democratic Donkey made their first appearance. Both were conceptions of Thomas Nast, based on the Fables of Aesop. Today's familiar images of Uncle Sam, John Bull, and Columbia also were conceived by Nast during this period.

Thomas Nast was a controversial character. Whereas the staunchly Republican Union League Club of New York honored him for his ardent devotion to the preservation of the Union, the New York *World* accused him of bigotry and pandering to the "meanest passions and prejudices of the most unthoughtful persons of the day." Obviously, one's opinion of the artist depended upon whether one agreed with his views or not. To him all things were either black or white. There was nothing in between. He was absolutely merciless in his attacks upon those with whom he disagreed. The Ku Klux Klan, anarchists, Communists, corrupt politicians, and even the Irish and the Catholic Church were among those upon whom he vented his wrath, while he vigorously supported, among other causes, sound money, the enfranchisement of Negroes, and the recognition of the rights of minority groups, including Indians and Chinese, and the conservation of wildlife. During this period Thomas Nast made his position known on every important national issue and to very telling effect. His cartoons attacking anarchy, Communism, and inflation are as appropriate today as when he drew them almost a century ago.

By 1877 Thomas Nast was a relatively wealthy man with an unusually good income in terms of that day. Not yet forty years old, he had just about everything that he could wish for—a nationwide reputation for integrity gained by supporting the things in which he believed, a lovely home, a devoted wife and family, and financial independence. Sarah Nast had contributed greatly to her husband's success, often reading to him as he worked. Shakespeare and the Bible were the inspirations for many of the artist's drawings and Sarah Nast supplied many of the ideas and captions for them. Mrs. Nast was a charming hostess and entertained her husband's prominent friends graciously and unostentatiously. General Grant and his wife and Mark Twain were guests on more than one occasion.

One family story is that at one formal dinner at the Nast home when General and Mrs. Grant were guests, daughters Edith and Mabel Nast, being too young to attend, but wishing to be in on the party, were decked out in maids' uniforms and served as waitresses. All went well until brother Tom Nast, Jr., who was old enough to be seated with the guests, started pinching his sisters each time they passed. The "wait-

The Cartoon that Captured Tweed.

resses' " reactions were such that the guests soon noticed that something unusual was going on. Finally, after the girls held a whispered conversation with their father complaining of young Tom's misbehavior, Thomas Nast introduced his daughters and the guests had a good laugh.

As the result of his national prominence, the artist received many attractive offers to appear on the lecture platform, few of which he accepted. It was an activity that he cordially disliked. For one thing, it kept him away from his home where he now did all of his work. Equally important was the fact that he suffered so from stage fright that he frequently became ill before an appearance.

Some offers were hard to refuse, such as one extended by the Boston Lyceum Bureau, offering ten thousand dollars for a ten-week tour. But at the time the artist was too busy with his assignments for *Harper's*, work which he much preferred. Two years later he was approached again being offered "a larger sum for a hundred lectures than any man living." But Nast again declined. Not long after, Mark Twain, a good friend, submitted a proposition in his characteristic humorous style. It read:

> My dear Nast:
>
> I did not think I should ever stand on a platform again until the time was come for me to say "I die innocent." But the same old offers keep arriving. I have declined them all, just as usual, though sorely tempted, as usual.
>
> Now I do not decline because I mind talking to an audience, but because (1) travelling alone is so heartbreakingly dreary, and (2) shouldering the whole show is such a cheer-killing responsibility.
>
> Therefore, I now propose to you what you proposed to me in November, 1867, ten years ago (when I was unknown, viz., that you stand on the platform and make pictures, and I stand by you and blackguard the audience. I should enormously enjoy meandering around (to big towns— I don't want to go to the little ones) with you for company.
>
> My idea is not to fatten the lecture agents and lyceums on the spoils, but put all the ducats religiously into two equal piles, and say to the artist and lecturer, "Absorb these." [Then followed a list of cities to be visited.]
>
> Call the gross receipts $100,000 for four months and a half and the profit from $60,000 to $75,000 (I try to make the figures large enough and leave it to the public to reduce them).
>
> I did not put in Philadelphia because P—— owns that town, and last winter when I made a little reading trip he only paid me $300 and pretended his concert (I read fifteen minutes in the midst of a concert)

"Thomas Nast was in favor of wildlife conservation."

Sarah Nast in 1877. Oil portrait by Thomas Nast.

cost him a vast sum, and so he couldn't afford any more. I could get up a better concert with a barrel of cats.

Well, think it over, Nast, and drop me a line. We should have some fun.

Yours truly,
Samuel L. Clemens

It seemed a fascinating plan, but again Nast had no inclination to leave his home and family, so regretted.

By 1879, Thomas Nast was beginning to get restive. Changes in management at *Harper's* had resulted in less freedom to express his own views. A new generation of publishers did not wholly agree with what they considered their artist's tendency to advocate startling and, in their opinion, sometimes radical reforms. Then too, with the introduction of new techniques in reproduction, the hand-engraved wood block, which Nast had used to such advantage, had become outmoded and the new methods were less suited to his style. Consequently, as Nast's drawings appeared less frequently in the *Weekly* he took advantage of the opportunity to travel and invest his savings. While Thomas Nast would have been the last to realize it, he had, at the age of thirty-nine, reached his peak.

Nast had learned little about finance during his career as an artist, as would soon become apparent. An investment in a silver mine in Colorado proved unprofitable and became a drain on his resources. But in 1883 his financial problems seemed about to be over. His good friend General U. S. Grant had, after retiring from the Presidency, invested all of his savings in a Wall Street firm headed by Ferdinand Ward, a Wall Street investment banker. U. S. Grant, Jr., who lacked financial experience, was made a junior partner to look after his father's interest. The venture prospered to such an extent, or so it appeared, judging by the dividends declared, that General Grant offered Nast an opportunity to participate, a privilege accorded to only a select few. This seemed the chance to recoup his mining losses, so the artist sold a piece of property and invested the proceeds in the firm of Grant and Ward. The generous dividends that ensued encouraged Nast to take his family abroad for a much needed rest.

It was not long after his return, however, that headlines in his morning paper announced that Grant and Ward had failed! It seemed incredible in view of the optimistic reports and liberal dividends he had been receiving. But the fact was that Ferdinand Ward had proven to be an unscrupulous manipulator who, in order to maintain the fiction of profitability, had been declaring dividends out of capital funds until there was no more capital left.

Nast Contemplating the "Bust" of Ward.

Ignisfatuus Wall Street.

Thomas Nast lost everything that he had invested, while General Grant lost even more. Grant had personally guaranteed one of the firm's notes a few days before the failure was announced and in order to help pay off the note had to sell everything he could get his hands on, including military trophies and souvenirs from all over the world. The later publication of his memoirs enabled Grant's family to meet all of his obligations.

The disenchantment that followed Nast's first and final experience in Wall Street was revealed in two of his pictures. One, a self-caricature in oil, depicts the artist's complete bewilderment and despair. The fact that he could so unmercifully portray himself after such a disaster, shows that one thing he had not lost was his sense of humor. Actually, the portrait was not painted until 1902, eighteen years after the Ward failure, evidence of the lasting impression the event had made on the artist. The original painting, on loan from the Smithsonian Institution, hung in the White House office of Daniel P. Moynihan during the time he served as Counselor to President Nixon. It was known among Dr. Moynihan's colleagues as "Nast Contemplating the 'Bust' of Ward."

Another picture recalling this tragic experience is Nast's scathing indictment of high finance entitled "Ignisfatuus Wall Street." It shows Satan and his skeleton-like companion on a swing suspended in a chasm formed by Wall Street's tall buildings. Their seat is a Board, suggestive of the Exchange's Board of Governors and the Ring around Satan's waist is reminiscent of Tweed's corrupt Ring. It would not be surprising if the artist's picture of the Devil resembled Ferdinand Ward!

Relations between Nast and *Harper's* did not improve during the Presidential campaign of 1884, when the cartoonist found himself unable to support James G. Blaine, the Republican candidate for the Presidency. For the first time Thomas Nast campaigned for a Democrat, caricaturing Blaine as "The Plumed Knight." Grover Cleveland, the Democratic candidate whom Nast supported, was elected.

Shortly thereafter, the artist journeyed West to investigate the mine in which his savings had been sunk. The mine proved to be a lost cause, but while in Colorado he was honored by having a lofty, snow-covered peak in the Rocky Mountains, named after him.

In 1886 came the end of Thomas Nast's association with *Harper's Weekly*, a magazine which he had made famous and in which he had made his fame. In the quarter-century of the Nast-*Harper's* relationship, the nation had passed through a turbulent period and Nast's drawings in the magazine would provide a vivid pictorial chronicle of those years. But in terminating his connection with *Harper's*, Nast had lost his forum, while at the same time the *Weekly* lost its political importance.

The opportunity to launch his own paper, dedicated to "Principles—Not Men," of which he had so long dreamed, came a few years later, but this venture was doomed to failure, leaving the artist heavily in debt. Nast consoled himself, however, that he had lost no one's money but his own. Now came the time when horses and carriages had to be sold, faithful servants dismissed, and a mortgage placed on the home.

It was like manna from heaven, therefore, when in 1889, his old friends at *Harper's* proposed that he get together a collection of his Christmas drawings for publication in book form, a very Christmas-like gesture and one which Nast gratefully accepted.

Thomas Nast's book of *Christmas Drawings for the Human Race* was published in time for the 1890 Christmas season. It contained pictures that had appeared in Christmas issues of *Harper's* over a period of thirty years as well as some drawn by him especially for inclusion in the book. The five Nast children were used as models in many of the drawings and many scenes from the Nast home were also incorporated.

It seemed fitting that the artist's last assignment for *Harper's* should be on a theme transcending the fortunes of politics, thus offering him an opportunity to devote his talents to a subject very close to his heart but which had been subordinated to his political activities. The title was especially significant in that the cartoonist who had formerly lampooned his adversaries with such vehemence, was now including all humans in his offering of Christmas good will, regardless of their race, creed, or political affiliation.

Clement Moore's poem was the inspiration for many of Thomas Nast's drawings. His picture of the "Night before Christmas" scene, with the mice asleep in their beds, is a delightful interpretation of Moore's opening lines and the drawing of Santa riding high above the moonlit rooftops in his reindeer-drawn sleigh, his ubiquitous pipe held aloft in a gesture of farewell as he heads back toward the North Pole, provides a fitting finale to the poem. Who would have believed that the cartoonist who had so viciously attacked Tweed and his Ring twenty years earlier, could be capable of creating such heart-warming pictures? But, whereas Moore described St. Nicholas as a "jolly old elf" with the "stump of a pipe held tight in his teeth," Nast preferred the long-stemmed clay pipes smoked by the Pelz-Nicol of his boyhood and the Sancte Klaas of Holland.

The artist's concept of Santa Claus had changed considerably since he first pictured him in camp in 1862. Santa now had flowing white locks and moustaches, a broad girth and captivating smile. He was the very embodiment of merriment and

Santa by the Fireplace. Painted by Nast about 1895.

" 'Twas the night before Christmas, and all through the house
Not a creature was stirring, *not even a mouse*."

"Merry Christmas to all, and to all a good-night."

good cheer, a far cry from the Old World versions of the past, such as Russia's St. Nicholas with his cope, crosier, and miter.

Santa Claus's workshop at the North Pole was also a product of Nast's imagination. Just why Santa Claus chose the North Pole as his base of operations has never been quite clear, but the chances are logistics had something to do with it. The North Pole was equidistant from most of the countries in the Northern Hemisphere that Santa visited. And it may be assumed that he wished to locate someplace where he could work without interruption and not be spied upon by inquisitive youngsters. Furthermore, as a resident of the North Pole, no country could claim him as a national. The North Pole workshop was a busy place and when Santa was not occupied in making toys he was on the lookout for good children with his telescope or recording their behavior in his voluminous account book, another of Nast's conceptions.

The picture, with its elaborate detail, is obviously from one of the artist's earlier woodcuts, the dwarf-like Santa resembling the one who distributed gifts to soldiers at the front in 1862. The sketch of Santa trimming the tree is one of the few drawings of this collection in which the Christmas tree appears. This seems strange, as decorating the Christmas tree was so much a part of Christmas in the artist's native Germany, where the custom originated.

The composite drawing presents an interesting catalog of toys so popular with children of that day, some of which present-day oldsters will remember with nostalgia: jumping jacks and jacks-in-the-box, hobbyhorses and cockhorses, toy soldiers, wooden animals, miniature houses and trees to be laid out in little villages, dolls with china heads and sawdust-filled bodies, dolly dresses and dollhouses with furniture for each room, tenpins, drums, tools, and building blocks—enough to keep Santa Claus busy all year long. Little wonder that he took time to relax before his open fire during the week following Christmas.

Santa Claus's benevolent spirit is apparent as he sits at his desk looking over his morning mail. And we just know that he is going to forgive those children whose misbehavior has been reported by their parents in the stack of letters piled high before him. Nast's Santa treated good and naughty children alike. He did not discriminate as did the original St. Nicholas who bestowed cookies and sweets on the good children and switches and rods on the naughty.

In addition to his records of behavior, Santa must have had an elaborate filing system to keep track of the requests made by children who wrote him directly, and it was the Santa created by Nast who read them all. Letters deposited in mailboxes must have reached him somehow, as the wishes of the young writers were usually

Santa Claus's Mail.

"Cookies and sweets for the good children, and
switches and rods for the naughty."

Christmas Post.

Messages and Lists for Santa Claus.

Old SANTECLAUS with much delight

His reindeer drives this frosty night,

O'er chimney tops, and tracks of snow,

To bring his yearly gifts to you.

filled. Other Christmas lists, intended for Santa but entrusted to the head of the family, may not have reached their destination but somehow Santa got the message and the desired presents were found under the tree on Christmas morning.

Although Clement Moore had placed St. Nicholas in a sleigh behind eight reindeer in 1822, he was not the first to associate a sleigh and reindeer with the good saint. As early as 1809, Washington Irving had described St. Nicholas as flying through the air in a reindeer-drawn sleigh and in 1821 a picture was published of Santa in a sleigh loaded with rewards behind a single reindeer, probably his first such appearance.

Professor Moore had been quick to seize upon the idea, increasing the number of reindeer from one to eight. And a motley team it was—Dasher and Dancer, Prancer and Vixen, Comet and Cupid, Donder and Blitzen—names drawn from the race tracks and hunting fields of England as well as the stables of Greek mythology, with a dash of German vernacular thrown in.

How realistic Thomas Nast made Santa appear as he illustrated Clement Moore's account of Santa's arrival on the housetop. Little wonder that children of his day listened for the tinkle of sleigh bells and the pawing of reindeer hoofs on the roof before they went off to sleep. In all of Nast's drawings of Santa shown with little children, one senses the intense excitement and feeling of anticipation that pervaded the air on Christmas Eve.

As evidenced by the number of drawings devoted to the subject, Thomas Nast loved the custom of hanging stockings by the fireplace, a tradition that had originated in Asia Minor fifteen hundred years earlier. It was then, according to legend, that Nicholas, the very real Bishop of Myra during the fourth century and later patron saint of Russia, started the custom.

The good Bishop, so the story goes, having heard of an impoverished nobleman who was unable to provide dowries for his three daughters and procure suitable marriages for them, took it upon himself to help the poor father in his predicament. The accounts vary as to just how this was done, but the most plausible one tells of how Nicholas visited the home of the poor maidens on two successive nights, dropping purses of gold down the chimney. On the third night, one of the daughters, not wishing to miss anything, hung her stocking by the fireplace to catch her purse. She was successful, thereby establishing a precedent for generations to come. Happily, all of the daughters found acceptable husbands, a custom was started, and Nicholas would later become the patron saint of unmarried girls, as well as sailors, children, scholars, bankers, and even thieves! The residents of the Bishop's diocese, impressed by his benevolence, themselves adopted the practice of dropping gifts down the chimneys of the poor.

" 'Twas the Night Before Christmas."
A chance to test Santa Claus's generosity.

Christmas Station.

Christkindchen.

St. Nicholas became the traditional bringer of gifts to children in Russia, making his rounds on his horse on the eve of his birthday, December 6. However, the practice was soon discouraged by the Church as being an escape from reality. Following St. Nicholas' liquidation as a gift bringer in Russia, his counterpart appeared in Germany during the sixteenth century, only to suffer the same fate. He became so popular that he was accused of drawing the attention of children away from the Christ Child. For a while thereafter St. Nicholas' place was taken by the German "Christkind," a mythical figure represented by a youth or a young girl, who distributed gifts but was never seen. Thomas Nast recalled the legend with his appealing drawing of the "Christkindchen."

But the Germans, who made so much of Christmas, were not long in creating their own successor to St. Nicholas. He was Pelz-Nicol, who, instead of coming on the night before St. Nicholas' birthday, made his rounds of children's homes on Christmas Eve. Thus the secular celebration, with its gift giving, was made to coincide with the religious observance of Christ's birth, a development from which the Church has never quite recovered.

Just how December 25 came to be fixed upon as Christ's birthday is debatable as there is really no way of knowing the exact day of the year on which this historic event took place. The fact is that there is not a single month in the year to which the Nativity was not assigned by early Christian writers. Consequently, we must either accept the date of December 25 as one of many guesses, or admit that the celebration of Christmas on that day had something to do with pagan tradition.

It was at the time of the winter solstice that the Romans of the Empire celebrated the ascension of the unconquered sun after its autumnal decline. What is more logical than that the Church should choose the same occasion, hoping to attract to the worship of the Son of God some of the adoration bestowed by pagans upon their sun god? Still others claim that the date finally decided upon had its origin in Rome's riotous Saturnalian festival or the celebration of the Roman Kalends, the former occurring a week before and the latter a week after December 25.

Most of Nast's Christmas drawings are enlivened with sprigs of holly, mistletoe, and evergreen boughs, such as had been used to decorate homes since early Roman days. They were symbols of everlasting life when all other forms of plant life were brown and dead. In ancient times holly was believed to have sacred characteristics and was used for divination. It found its way to America as a Christmas decoration by way of England. Then, too, the holly wreath, with its thorns and blood-red berries, is quite logically associated with the Passion of Christ.

Mistletoe, in several European countries, was thought to have powers to cure

CHRISTMAS GREENS.

"So now is come our joyful'st feast—
Let every man be jolly;

Each room with ivy leaves is cheer'd,
And every post with holly."

Cutting Mistletoe in the South.

sickness and make barren animals fertile, no doubt owing to the fact that in early Celtic speech, "mistletoe" meant "all healer." Pliny, the Roman author of the first century, described the important part mistletoe played in an ancient Druidic ceremony. According to his account, a white-robed Druid climbed a sacred oak and cut the mistletoe with a golden sickle. As a sprig fell to the ground it was caught in a white cloth and two white bulls were sacrificed with prayer. The mistletoe-cutting procedure in Thomas Nast's drawing would appear far less complicated and equally effective.

The practice of kissing under the mistletoe was originally related to the spirit of fertility associated with the sacred bough. According to Washington Irving, young men in the England of his day plucked a berry every time they kissed a girl. When the berries were all gone, the privilege ceased. In Thomas Nast's "Christmas Flirtation" his eldest daughter Julia, aware of the legend or no, has chosen a sprig of mistletoe well-laden with berries beneath which to stand.

Many of the customs that characterize Christmas in America today originated in Nast's native Germany. It was there in 1605 that fir trees were first set up in parlors and were decorated with "roses, cut out of many-colored paper, apples, wafers, gold foil, sweets, and etc." Again, in Germany, we find in 1737, the first recorded mention of candles being used to decorate the tree. The illuminated tree, known as the *Weihnachtsbaum,* was a thing of wonder by night with its glittering ornaments and countless shining lights, symbolic, according to legend, of the starry heavens above Bethlehem on that first Christmas Eve. The custom spread to other European countries and in 1840 Queen Victoria of England was introduced to the Christmas tree by Prince Albert, her German-born consort. It was not long thereafter that it found its way to America.

While the celebration of Christmas has followed somewhat the same pattern in Christian countries throughout the world, each nation has fashioned its own festivities, characteristic of the people themselves.

In England, church ceremonies are followed by home festivals in which Father Christmas, the British counterpart of Santa Claus, plays a part. It is a season of good will among classes, reflecting the early days when the lord of the castle received everyone. It is a time for the enjoyment of solid material comforts. The spirit of the day is nowhere better portrayed than in Dickens' *Christmas Carol.*

In the Scandinavian countries elaborate preparations are begun weeks in advance, with housecleaning, decorating with greens, and cooking of breads, cakes, cookies, and special meats. Festivities begin on Christmas Eve with the lighting of Yule candles and an elaborate supper. The family celebration, with its singing of carols,

Christmas Flirtation.

centers around the tree, under which presents are piled high. Use of animal masks and straw puppets in Scandinavian celebrations dates back to pagan festivals.

Christmas is celebrated in the Netherlands and Belgium with churchgoing and family gatherings in the home. Children leave their hay-filled shoes outside their doors for Sancte Klaas's horse.

The French place emphasis on the religious aspects of Christmas, with crèches in both church and home. Midnight mass on Christmas Eve is followed by an elaborate supper. It is a time of happy family reunions. Père Noël looks after the interests of children. Celebration of the *jour de l'an,* or French New Year's Day, is a more secular occasion.

Christmas is a sacred holiday in Italy with solemn ceremonies in churches and midnight mass. Here also the *Presèpio,* a miniature manger representative of the Nativity, is featured. Its Bambino is the center of attention, before which candles are lighted, musicians play, and guests kneel. Flowers take the place of evergreens, as decorations.

Few countries enjoy a more delightful celebration than Mexico, with its combination of religion and amusement. Every home is decorated with flowers, while *posadas* are featured. These processions, bearing images of Joseph and Mary, commemorate their wanderings in search of shelter on Christmas Eve in Bethlehem.

Although Christmastime is associated with frost and snow in northern countries, December is a summer month below the equator. Thus, in Brazil Christmas is celebrated in midsummer. There is much gaiety as befits the Latin-American temperament, including fiestas, fireworks, and processions with flower-covered floats. Some North American customs have crept in, including the Christmas tree, the hanging of stockings, and Papa Noel, a Brazilian version of Santa Claus with his reindeer and sleigh.

Children in Syria leave food and drink for the tiny camel that accompanied the Wise Men, while in Puerto Rico children go to great trouble to place boxes on rooftops on Christmas Eve in hopes of having Santa fill them with gifts.

Christmas in the United States reflects the customs of the many countries of which it is the melting pot. But there is a common denominator in the celebrations of Christmas wherever held throughout the world. It is the one day, above all others, when Peace and Good Will ring in the air and Santa Claus does his part to keep the bells pealing.

Thomas Nast, like most Germans, retained some of that unpretentious and warm-hearted spirit of youth that enabled him to enter into the spirit of Christmas with childlike delight. In the words of Dickens, "he knew how to keep Christmas well."

Each Christmas Eve he arranged presents around the candle-lit family tree in original and unconventional ways. There was always a multitude of marvelously big and elaborate paper dolls that the artist father had cut out and arranged in processions marching in and out among the larger presents.

The practice of giving presents at Christmastime dates back to early Roman days, if, in fact, it did not originate almost two thousand years ago with the gifts of gold, frankincense, and myrrh brought to the manger in Bethlehem by the Wise Men. In Rome, during the Empire, "men gave honeyed things that the year of the recipient might be full of sweetness; lamps that it might be full of light; copper and gold that wealth might flow amain."

There is no record of the sending of Christmas cards before 1843 and it was not until 1862 that the exchange of greeting cards became general. Thomas Nast in later years sent out many original sketches to his friends with compliments of the season.

Nast's First Prize Christmas Card—being farthest from the subject

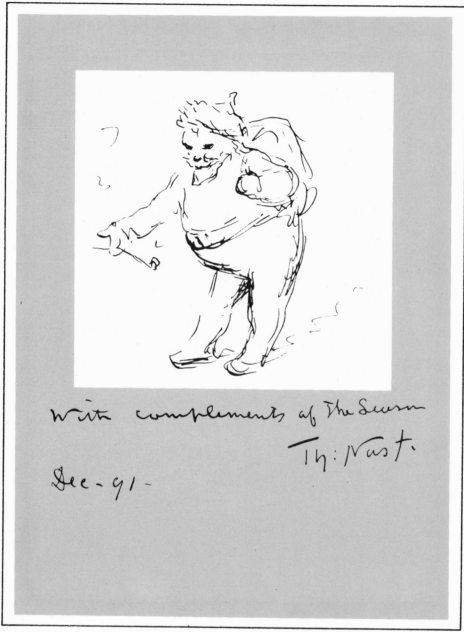

with complements of the Season

Th: Nast.

Dec - 91 -

Nast's Santa Claus Greeting Card.

One might wonder how Mother Goose pictures got into a book about Christmas. Probably for no other reasons than that Mother Goose and Santa Claus were parts of the same world of make-believe and Mother Goose, like Santa, was loved by little children and that was all that mattered to the artist. Furthermore, a more compatible couple could scarcely be imagined.

But who was Mother Goose? And where did she come from? That depends upon which tale of her origin we choose to accept. Both the Old and the New Worlds claim her as their own. There is little doubt that Mother Goose was a real person, but whether she was the Queen of Sheba or Queen Bertha, the mother of Charlemagne, as some Old World authorities would have us believe, or America's Elizabeth Foster Goose, mother of sixteen and grandmother of many more, who lived in Boston during the first half of the eighteenth century, is a moot question. But before taking sides, we should understand that most of the tales attributed to Mother Goose are actually much older than she. Mother Goose was, after all, a teller of tales, not a composer. And some of these tales, according to scholarly researchers, have meanings of far greater significance than the simple nursery rhymes themselves.

For example, according to legend, the plum that Little Jack Horner is seen plucking out of the Christmas pie in Nast's drawing, as four drooling dogs look on, relates to an incident during the reign of Henry VIII of England, early in the sixteenth century. According to this account, Thomas Horner, a steward of England's Glastonbury Cathedral, was entrusted by the Abbot to deliver a Christmas gift to the king. It was a pie containing the deeds to twelve manorial estates. But before presenting the pie to the king, Horner, so the story goes, extracted for himself the finest plum of all, the deed to the manor of Mells, where his descendants live to this day.

And theories abound about the "Sing-a-Song-of-Sixpence" rhyme. It has been suggested that the blackbirds are the twenty-four hours of the day, the king the sun, and the queen the moon. Still others have identified the king as Henry VIII, the queen as Katherine, and the maid as Anne Boleyn, while the twenty-four blackbirds, like the plums in Jack Horner's pie, were manorial deeds.

Both of these rhymes were favorites of Thomas Nast and were prominent not only in his Christmas drawings but in the decorative tiles that surround the fireplaces in his Morristown home.

Thomas Nast's *Christmas Drawings for the Human Race* portray all of these tales, customs, and traditions, and vividly recall those precious moments of Christmas Eves

A Merry Christmas.

Little Jack Horner.

long past, when stockings were hung by the fireplace and children rushed on Christmas morning to see the presents that had been left under the tree. And may we not forget that it is still true, as it was a century and a quarter ago, when Charles Dickens wrote his immortal *Christmas Carol* that "it is good to be children sometimes and never better than at Christmas, when its mighty Founder was a child himself."

Thomas Nast's
CHRISTMAS DRAWINGS

FOR

THE HUMAN RACE

NEW YORK · HARPER & BROTHERS   PRINTERS &
PUBLISHERS · FRANKLIN SQUARE   M DCCC XC

SANTA CLAUS.

MERRY CHRISTMAS

MERRY OLD SANTA CLAUS.

"HELLO! SANTA CLAUS!"

"HELLO! LITTLE ONE!"

THE SHRINE OF ST. NICHOLAS.—"We are all good children."

SANTA CLAUS'S ROUTE.

CHRISTMAS EVE.—Santa Claus waiting for the children to get to sleep.

SEEING SANTA CLAUS.

"SANTA CLAUS CAN'T SAY THAT I'VE FORGOTTEN ANYTHING."

THE WATCH ON CHRISTMAS EVE.

CHRISTMAS FANCIES.—"Don't you wish you wore stockings?"

DARNING THE STOCKINGS.

THE CRUSTY OLD BACHELOR
WHO IS BOUND TO HAVE SOMETHING IN HIS STOCKING.

RECIPROCATION.

"Won't Santa Claus be surprised to find that he has not been forgotten?"

A VERY BAD BOY.

THE COMING OF SANTA CLAUS.

"ANOTHER STOCKING TO FILL."

CAUGHT!

SANTA CLAUS'S REBUKE.

"I'll never do it again."

A CHRISTMAS BOX.

"For he's a jolly good fellow, so say we all of us."

MERRY CHRISTMAS.

CHRISTMAS EVE.—OLD FACES FOR YOUNG HEARTS.

"HERE WE ARE AGAIN!"

A CHRISTMAS SKETCH.—"Five o'clock in the morning."

THE DOMESTIC EXPRESS.

Old Bachelor: "How glad I am that I don't have to cart round
endless bundles for greedy brats during the holidays."

"WHO SAID ANYTHING ABOUT CHRISTMAS DINNER?"

"COME NOW, SANTA CLAUS, I'S READY."

NURSERY TILES.—"There he is."

A CHRISTMAS STORY.—"I am Cinderella, and you are the wicked sisters."

SEE! THE CHRISTMAS PLUM PUDDING.

THE CHRIST CHILD.

THE DEAR LITTLE BOY THAT THOUGHT CHRISTMAS CAME OFTENER.

SANTA CLAUS'S TOOL-BOX.

MOVING DAY.

'TWAS THE NIGHT AFTER CHRISTMAS.

"Wishing you a Merry Christmas and a Happy New Year."

OLD MOTHER GOOSE MELODIES.

"Little Bo-Peep fell fast asleep, and dreampt—"

THE SAME OLD CHRISTMAS STORY OVER AGAIN.

Epilogue

Of the several books that have been written in recent years about Thomas Nast and his art, it is this grandson's opinion that this republication of his favorite Christmas drawings would have pleased him most of all. Long after the political campaigns in which he participated became part of history and his battles against corruption in high places had ended, the spirit of Christmas continued to occupy a very special place in his heart.

My earliest recollections of my grandfather relate to the many times that I visited the Morristown home in the years just before and just after the turn of the century. I was fortunate in being a favorite of his as a boy, no doubt because my mother, who was Edith Nast, was very close to her father and I was his eldest grandson.

Following the publication of his *Christmas Drawings* in 1890, my grandfather spent a great deal of his time in his studio at home, painting. He seemed to find peace and relaxation in quietly working on his canvases. The days of the crusading cartoonist who sometimes dipped his pen in vitriol were past. Thomas Nast the painter was a gentler person and the only one whom this grandson ever knew.

Most of the painter's pictures had to do with Civil War subjects, many of them being based on sketches he had made on the scene thirty years earlier. His huge canvas showing New York's famous Seventh Regiment marching down Broadway on its way to war in April of 1861 and his "Peace in Union" painting depicting the surrender scene at Appomattox four years later, have been widely reproduced and are recognized for their authenticity. In a different vein were his "Immortal Light of Genius," a tribute to William Shakespeare, a replica of which hung in the Shakespeare Memorial at Stratford on Avon, England. It was stored during enemy bombing attacks in World War II and was irreparably damaged. Thomas Nast's "Head of Christ," acquired by J. Pierpont Morgan, was loaned by Morgan to the Metropolitan Museum of Art in New York City, where it was once shown.

Had Thomas Nast followed his early aspiration to become a painter, he might well have earned recognition in that field rather than as a cartoonist. As it was, his training was not such as to gain him the reputation in the field of art that he was to win in caricature. Critics have acknowledged that his paintings, while they appear labored, have a heavy power and deserve more recognition than they have received.

Most of my grandfather's paintings were commissioned by old friends and, while payments were liberal, income from this source was insufficient to support his family.

Thomas Nast.

Thomas Nast and his Two Grandsons, Thomas Nast St. Hill
and Thomas Nast Crawford.

During his painting years, the artist often hung his paintings next to a large window to dry in the sun, sometimes upside down or sideways. Included among these were his self-caricature and his head of Christ. On one occasion during this period the delivery of my grandfather's daily paper was suddenly discontinued. Upon complaining to the distributor he learned that the young boy who delivered the papers had seen what he thought to be strange people looking out of the window. The paper boy concluded that the house was haunted and when he finally saw the Lord himself peering out of the window, he was definitely through and would deliver no more papers to that house!

Of course, I was not old enough to appreciate that my grandfather was having

"There was something of the actor in Thomas Nast."

financial problems, but I later learned that it distressed him that he was unable to be as generous to his family and friends as he had been during his more affluent years.

I recall Thomas Nast as a relatively short man, perhaps five foot six or seven, always impeccably dressed in dark jacket with boutonniere, waistcoat with gold watch chain, a stickpin in his ascot tie, and gray striped trousers such as are worn with a cutaway. He was very distinguished looking with his gray hair, which was always tousled, his Vandyke beard, and flowing moustaches. He wore a wide-brimmed fedora hat and carried a silver-headed cane, which he often tucked under his arm as he strode along. There was something of the actor in him and he was, in fact, a member of The Players, a club in New York whose roster included most of the leading actors of the day, as well as some artists and musicians.

My grandfather took me to the club on several occasions but I cannot say that I recall any of the stage celebrities I met there. Strange as it may seem, the character I most clearly recall from those visits was the traffic policeman at a busy intersection nearby. The officer tipped his helmet and greeted my grandfather by name as we crossed the street together, whereupon we stopped in the middle of the crowded thoroughfare as I was introduced. A very proud moment!

From time to time my grandfather took me to the theatre or circus in New York, and on one such occasion I recall going backstage to meet the famous actor, Joseph Jefferson, who played Rip in *Rip van Winkle*. I was even more impressed that Buffalo Bill was a friend. I can still recall the shooting of the cowboys and the yelping of the Indian warriors in Buffalo Bill's exciting Wild West Show. And I remember seeing Annie Oakley shoot clay pigeons from every conceivable posture. The show was presented in Madison Square Garden, and I wondered why the bullets from Annie Oakley's gun didn't kill some of the audience, not realizing that she used a shotgun, not a rifle. Tickets to most of the performances we attended together were free passes, known at the time as "Annie Oakleys," owing to the fact that they had holes punched in them, as though perforated by Annie's shotgun.

Among the most treasured souvenirs of my relationship with my grandfather are three sketches commemorating our first "Spree" together. I was seven years old at the time. The first of these, sent on Valentine's Day, 1902, announced in rhyme that we were to go on a spree the following Wednesday. My mother had arranged to provide the necessary funds for the outing. The next sketch, five days later, is a wordless message that speaks for itself. It shows my grandfather sitting on the edge of his chair, hat on, cane in hand, ready and eager to be off. But the dollar sign and the question mark on his traveling bag tell the story. The check has not arrived! The

DEAR BUD -
I LOVE YOU - AND YOU LOVE ME!
WE WILL GO ON A SPREE
NEXT WEDNES-DAY
IT DOES NOT RHYME - BECAUSE IT'S ALL REASON.
Jennys St. Thomas Valentine . Feb 14 - 1902 .

problem was apparently solved before the big day, however, as the final sketch shows us marching joyfully down the street after attending a matinee at the Broadway Theatre. The reference to our first spree having been "done up Brown" refers to our luncheon at Brown's, a well-known New York chophouse for men at the time.

That Thomas Nast was conscious of his short stature is evidenced by the caricatures he sometimes drew of himself standing on something to give him height. In one such cartoon he showed himself on a chair delivering a speech. The occasion was a Canvas-Back Club dinner at Harvey's Restaurant in Washington, D.C. He had become separated from his baggage on the train and was obliged to appear in his business suit instead of white tie and tails, which accounts for the caption on the drawing. This cartoon, together with one he drew of his host, the late George W. Harvey, still hangs on the wall of the famous Washington restaurant. Mr. Harvey once stated that he had several times refused offers of a thousand dollars for the drawings.

Other sketches that I prize highly reveal Thomas Nast's cleverness and sense of humor. Before I was old enough to write I sometimes enclosed in my mother's letters to her father pictures that I had drawn myself. They showed no evidence that I had inherited any of the artist's talent! Several of my drawings were returned after my grandfather had incorporated them in sketches of his own, such as the one in which he made my drawing appear on an easel before which he stood appraising the work of his latest "Rival in the Art Field." Others were similarly returned, showing his shocked incredulity on viewing his grandson's art. And when I was unable to draw a fish he made a sketch of the fish drawing me.

Thomas Nast's original sketches were highly valued by recipients and they often took the place of formal correspondence. He blamed his reluctance to write on his pen, which he said, did not know how to spell! He was a notoriously bad speller and sometimes mistakes crept into his captions, such as "Budy" for "Buddy," my childhood nickname, in the fish sketch. Fortunately, Sarah Nast corrected most of his misspelled captions before they appeared.

I remember seeing my grandfather at work in his home studio. I recall particularly the three-foot-high bronze statue of "The Gladiator" above his rolltop desk and the mockingbird in the cage close by. As I now realize, the statue of "The Gladiator" was symbolic, in that it represented one who, like Thomas Nast himself, engaged in fierce combat or controversy. The studio was on the second floor and as the mockingbird heard its master's footsteps ascending the stairs it would whistle to him and receive a whistle in reply. The bird had quite a repertoire and always responded to the attention paid to him by repeating the sounds he heard. When the artist was busy and had not taken notice of his feathered friend for some time, it would pick up a piece of gravel from the bottom of the cage and throw it at him.

My recollections of Villa Fontana as it was seventy years ago are still very clear. It was an imposing three-story house with mansard roof and widow's walk, set well back from the street from which it was hidden by tall evergreen trees. It was in one of Morristown's better residential neighborhoods but, at the time, sadly in need of

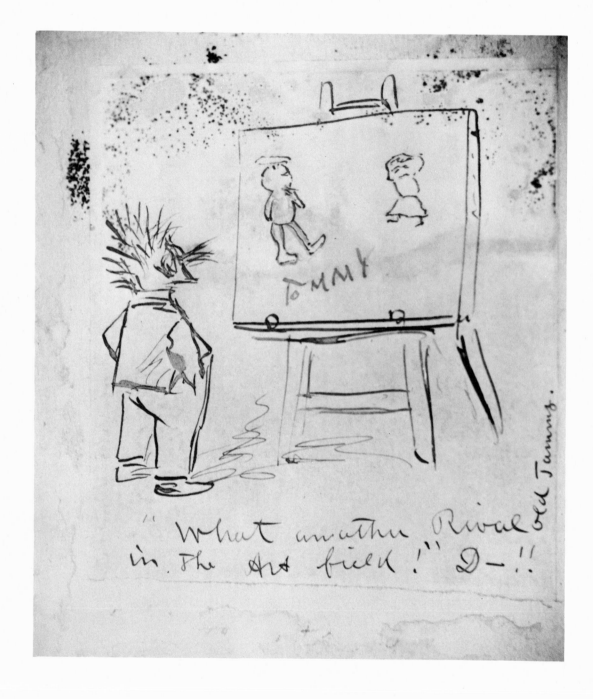

Help! Oh Help!
TOMMY

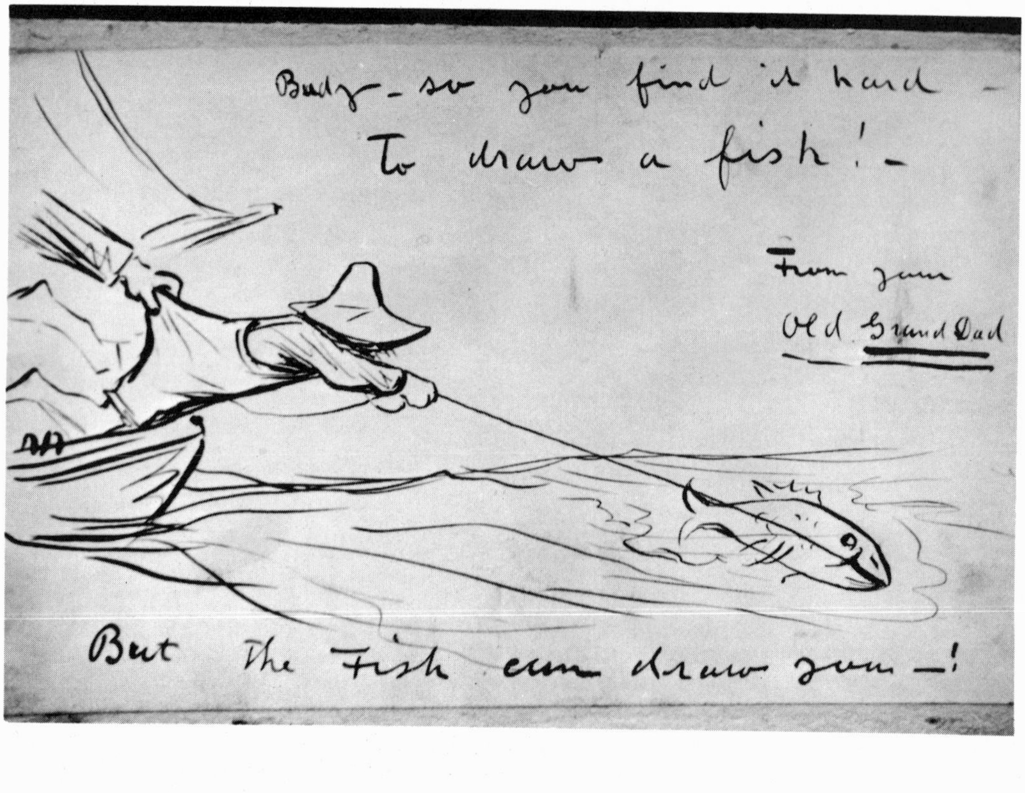
Budz—so you find it hard—
To draw a fish!—
From your
Old Grand Dad
But the Fish can draw you—!

paint. The fountain, for which the home was named, was beside the driveway that led to the front entrance, but it was dry when I played in it as a boy. Large brown toads hopped about among the dead leaves that covered the bottom of the pool's big round basin. The heavy rustic gate across the driveway was closed and its hinges were rusty. It had not been opened since General Grant's carriage drove out in 1883. The inside of the house was somber, with curtains drawn in all rooms not being used. Certain memories of childhood remain very vivid and I recall especially the steamy atmosphere of the gas-lit second-floor bathroom as boiling hot water poured out of the faucet into the wood-encased, copper-lined bathtub, the height of elegance in Victorian plumbing fixtures. The fireplaces were surrounded by tiles depicting the artist's favorite Mother Goose rhymes and Fables of Aesop. The motto "Time and Tide Wait for No Man," carved above one fireplace mantel, was beyond my comprehension but made a lasting impression on me.

Thomas Nast loved everything in nature, often staying up late at night to watch the stars and explain astronomy to his children. A story was told about the time that he was sitting with a group before an open fire in a warm room at The Players one cold wintry day and asked his friends if they would like to go out with him to see a great sight. Only one hardy soul cared to brave the weather. They had walked a few blocks when my grandfather stopped before a large plate-glass window covered with frost crystals. This was the great sight! His friend at first thought it was a joke, but was soon convinced that the artist was deadly serious and had to admit that it was beautiful.

In his younger days Thomas Nast had enjoyed horseback riding and walking, although his riding days were over when I knew him. He loved animals, particularly cats, greyhounds, pugs, and terriers, as evidenced by their prominence in his drawings. When one of his dogs was poisoned he was so distressed that he could not eat. This was the same man that was accused by his detractors as having a heart of stone.

My memories of my grandmother, Sarah Nast, during these days are equally strong. I recall her as a lovely, even-tempered lady who maintained her patrician bearing as she went quietly about her work presiding over the servantless Nast household. I never heard her speak a complaining or cross word, even during the later years when she was to make a home for me after my mother's death. I was fourteen years old at the time and my grandmother was in her middle seventies. She saw me through a very trying period until I was ready to go away to college. I still remember the times when we were invited to dine with my Uncle Cyril and his wife, who lived nearby. I was a prodigious milk drinker and in order to make sure that I enjoyed my daily ration, my grandmother would, to my embarrassment, carry with her a large pitcher of milk, holding it before her in order not to spill any as we walked along the city street together. Sarah Nast died at the age of ninety-two, outliving her husband by thirty years.

Would that I had asked my grandmother the many questions about my grandfather to which I would now like to have the answers. But, as Catherine Drinker Bowen wrote in her delightful *Family Portrait,* one seldom begins to care about one's ancestors until reaching the age of fifty.

What bothered my grandfather most as the century came to a close, was that he was heavily in debt. But he was not one to complain, even though he sometimes had to rely upon his talents to pay his doctor, dentist, and lawyer by painting their portraits for them. I was told that he once paid a tax collector in this manner, although how the collector settled with the taxing authority is not quite clear.

Thus it was, in 1901, when Theodore Roosevelt succeeded to the Presidency of the United States. Roosevelt, himself a fighter for the things in which he believed, had long admired a similar spirit in Thomas Nast and, wishing to do something to help him in his adversity, offered him an appointment as Consul General in Ecuador, South America. The offer was made in a letter from Secretary of State John Hay, advising that unfortunately this was the only post available at the time. "The President," Hay wrote, "would like to put it at your disposition, but if you think it too far away and too little amusing to a man with the soul of an artist, please say so frankly, and he will keep you in mind if anything better should turn up; but it is heartbreaking business waiting for vacancies. Our service is so edifying and preservative that few die and nobody resigns."

It was not an assignment that appealed to my grandfather, involving, as it did, business duties for which he was not at all qualified. But desperately in need of funds, the four-thousand-dollar-a-year stipend seemed a godsend to the artist who in his heyday had earned that much in a single month. He gratefully accepted the offer. It was a case of any port in a storm.

At the time he was notified of his appointment Thomas Nast was working on a painting of the defeated General Robert E. Lee as he awaited the arrival of General Grant at Appomattox Court House. It was to be called "The Hour of Surrender." The painting was never finished, but a photograph was taken of the artist as he stood before his painting, palette in hand. No doubt the disappointments experienced in later life had better enabled Thomas Nast to understand the anguish suffered by the great Southern leader. Looking at the photograph, one wonders which looks the sadder, the artist or the General. It was the hour of surrender for both.

When the time drew near for his departure for Ecuador the Consul-to-be got off one of his clever sketches advising Secretary Hay that he was ready to go.

The Hour of Surrender.
Nast with his portrait of General Lee at Appomattox.

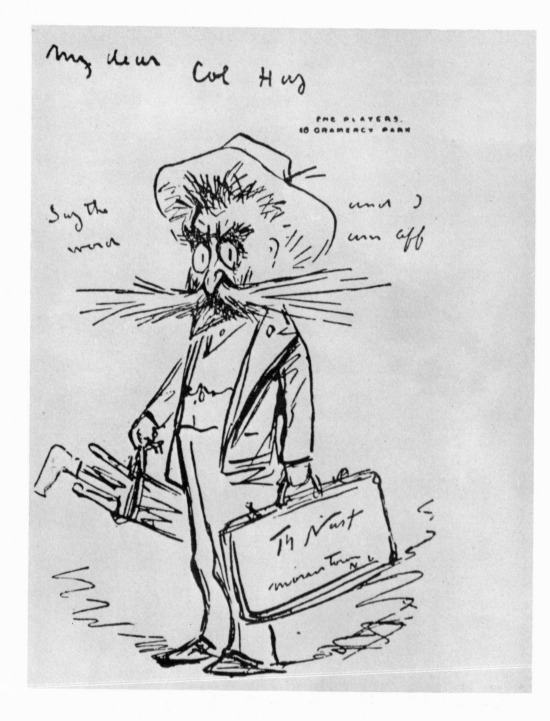

Guayaquil, the principal port in Ecuador, where the Consulate was located, had recently been ravaged by fire and the climate would have been difficult for a much younger man to endure. Nast was sixty-two years old at the time. In addition, sanitary conditions were poor and yellow fever was prevalent. When a friend asked my grandfather why he was going to such a forsaken spot, he replied that he wanted to learn how to pronounce the name of the place.

One of the attributes that had contributed so much to Thomas Nast's success as a political cartoonist was his uncanny ability to foresee future events. The same characteristic was now manifest as he left for his new post. Among the sketches that he handed out to reporters as his ship was about to sail was one of himself shaking with trepidation as he stood on the red-hot equator, while Yellow Jack, symbolic of yellow fever popped out of a box and pestilential fumes poured out of a volcano in the background.

My grandfather departed from New York by steamer in July, 1902, convinced, as revealed in a sketch that he left behind, that he would never return. He sailed without friends or family to see him off. He could not bear the thought of such a parting.

The letters he wrote home to my grandmother were sad, yet so illustrative of his true character that it seems fitting to quote from some of them. Here was a man who had known the good things of life—a devoted family, a lovely home, a host of friends, and the esteem of his countrymen—living out his life in a pesthole in order to pay off his obligations.

Shortly after his arrival in Guayaquil late in July he wrote home to his wife: "I don't know what I am about, really. The fire, the yellow fever and the dirt do not help to clear one's mind." Again, on August 3:

> Things are really working very slowly. I have a bath but no water yet. The cry is "tomorrow, tomorrow" and their tomorrow is longer in coming than in the States. I am still well, but the people here say that I shall be laid up with a chill. . . .
>
> They told me to be careful of the night air. Can't see how it can be kept out. There is not a pane of glass in the whole city. . . . The river is so close . . . when the tide is out the smell is in; when it comes back again, it washes the smell away.
>
> The picture of you and the grandchildren is up. As I look at it . . . I laugh too. It does seem funny that I am here, but my greatest happiness is that you are not here. . . .

The picture referred to was a photograph taken in 1898 on the steps of the Morristown home. My grandmother, Sarah Nast, grinning like a Cheshire cat, is surrounded

by her five grandchildren. Attired in sailor suit, with bosun's whistle in my pocket, I am seated in the front row between my two cousins, Muriel Nast Crawford (the late Mrs. Donald E. Battey), on my right, and on my left, in ruffled dress and flower-bedecked hat, her brother, the late John William Roy Crawford, Jr., both children of Mabel Nast Crawford. Thomas Nast Crawford, the youngest of the Crawford children, and the only one to inherit any of his grandfather's artistic ability, is seated on his grandmother's lap. My sister Edith, eldest of the grandchildren, is on the right in the back row. She died of diphtheria two years later. It was a happy group and little wonder that my grandfather laughed too as he looked at it. It added a cheery note to his otherwise dreary surroundings.

Two other grandchildren, Sarah Nast and Thomas Nast III, children of Cyril Nast, had not been born when this picture was taken. The only surviving grandchildren of Thomas and Sarah Nast are Thomas Nast III and myself.

118

Sarah Nast and Her Grandchildren.
A picture which made Nast laugh, too.

Conditions did not improve in Guayaquil. On August 12, my grandfather wrote home:

> Am well that's all. . . . About four dead as near as I can make out, but the doctors say it is genuine yellow fever. . . . Mice, rats, bats, mosquitoes, fleas, spiders, and dirt all thrive. Water scarce I haven't had a real bath yet. There is not enough to fill the tub. . . . Have to buy bed, mattress, pillows, sheets and so forth, and set up housekeeping myself. I don't think I can stand boarding.
>
> Oh—the people are very poor . . . no work, nothing doing. I am so glad no one else came.

How he must have yearned for the comforts of his home, including the steaming water in his copper-lined bathtub!

August 21.

A month ago I took charge of this office . . . only a month—heavens! How long it seems! Well, I must make the best of it. I hate the place, but don't say anything about that!

Yellow fever was now so rampant that ships from the north carrying mail no longer stopped at Guayaquil. Sometimes they dropped off the mail on their return trip from southern ports. It was exasperating to the consul to see a steamer in the stream unable to put ashore the letters from home which he knew must be aboard.

August 27.

It would go hard indeed with me if it were not for the Ashtons [Mr. Ashton was the British Vice-Consul], because one needs somebody—in case— well—trouble of any kind. But I must not give in. If sticking will do it, stick I will. It does bring more money than I can make at home, and time may do something, too.

September 15.

I think I am too old to catch the fever. I have a little hope left. Let's stick it out for another year, anyway.

September 21.

You say my poor old mockingbird misses me. I am very sorry. I do miss him, poor fellow, and his mocking sounds.

September 25.

This change has done me good in spite of everything. It is true there is a great deal of fever in this place, but I hope I shall escape it. They look at me and say "Well, you have not blue eyes. You are more like a native, and you are too old to catch it." What a blessing to be old. One is going to the next world soon anyway, so one is exempt. For the first time I feel glad that I am old.

September 29.

Everything is quiet. The so-called "best people" have made their exists on account of the yellow fever. The steamers do not stop here. They go south. That alarms people still more.

October 13.

Every day from two to four cases of yellow fever. Nearly all fatal. The Germans have the hardest time. . . . I can save more money now as I don't have dinner at night any more. At first I had to, I was so hungry.

Now that steamers had ceased to call at the port of Guayaquil because of the yellow-fever scare there was little for the American Consul to do. His job involved representing his government in all matters of trade and when there was no trade, time hung heavily on his hands.

October 20.

Well, well, what with painting, when I am able to do it (it dries so very slowly) and what with the Encyclopaedia Britannica, I manage to kill time. I have been reading it steadily and enjoy it very much. Knowledge is a great thing, but what a nuisance to find out how little we know, no matter how long we live and how much we study.

October 21.

Your letter just came. You say you have nothing to write, but write any-thing, even about the October days, the turning of the leaves. It makes me homesick, but I'd rather be homesick than have any other kind of sickness. Most of the people here look as if they were already dead.

Then follow reports of several friends and associates who have succumbed to the fever.

And then came what was probably the saddest letter of all, dated November 21, 1902:

You say the money arrived safely and it is in the bank. Just think of it! Bills paid and money, real money, in the bank again. . . . And so Mr. T—— thinks I should get a leave of absence from a place where I am making money? No, I must stick it out, no matter what takes place. I do think that I am making an impression, too, on the State Department. They have sent no complaints at all, and they may promote me, at least I hope so—and leave of absence would cost too much. I must stick. Now my job is all right, if we only get a little money ahead.

November 27.

I am anxious to hear from you—something to be thankful for on Thanks-giving Day. . . .

121

There was but one letter after this, a brief note on Sunday, November 30. The following day he complained of a little nausea, and by Saturday doctors pronounced his case as the fever in its worst form. On Sunday, December 7, he died, far from home and loved ones.

In his rolltop desk in the Morristown home was found the prophetic sketch made before his departure for Ecuador. It was a picture of his drawing materials, ink, pencil and pen, all tied together with black ribbon. He had had a premonition that he would never use them again.

A Sketch Found in Nast's Desk in Morristown after His Death.

L'Envoi

The little lad of Landau, who had left his native Germany fifty-six years before for America, had run his course in his adopted country. And now his work was finished.

I like Albert Bigelow Paine's eulogy in the closing paragraphs of his biography of my grandfather.

> Often in the hour of his elevation, he was charged with arrogance, self-assurance, and conceit. Yet these were never his characteristics. It was not self-assurance, but self-assuredness; not self-conceit, but self-certainty; not arrogance, but a proud impatience with anything that savored of surrender or compromise.
>
> Thomas Nast was a genius of the people and for the people, and his impress shall not perish from the world of art. Yet it may be that generations of the future will not write him down as an artist. Even so, to have been named by thoughtful and sincere men with Lincoln and Grant as a benefactor of his people, to have placed a great city in his eternal debt and to have died in his country's service, may perhaps be counted enough. He was often charged with being partisan, and this is a title which I think we may accept with honor. I think when the day comes, as it surely will, that men shall raise a tablet to his memory, then reverently we may inscribe upon it:
>
> THOMAS NAST, PATRIOT AND MORALIST
> A PARTISAN OF THE RIGHT

Paine's words were written in 1904, and half a century later, as he had predicted, the United States Embassy marked the military barracks in Landau, Bavaria, where Thomas Nast was born, with a bronze plaque, a bas-relief bust of the artist, with an inscription noting that it was a "gift to the German people in friendship and in memory of Thomas Nast." The week following the presentation was celebrated as Nast Week, the one-hundred-sixteenth anniversary of his birth. And a few years later, another bronze tablet was placed by the United States Department of the Interior on Thomas Nast's home in Morristown, designating it a registered Historic Landmark. Outside the grounds, next to the street curb, is a sign telling passersby that from 1872 to 1902 this was the home of Thomas Nast, who exposed the Tweed Ring and created the Republican Elephant and Democratic Donkey.

Across the street is Macculloch Hall, a beautiful Colonial home restored and maintained as a museum by the W. Parsons Todd Foundation. The museum includes a Nast Room containing a unique collection of the artist's work as well as the handsome Army and Navy Vase presented to my grandfather after the close of the Civil War by several thousand officers and enlisted men of the Army and Navy in recognition of the patriotic use he had made of his rare talent. The grounds of Villa Fontana are now well-kept and the house is freshly painted, scarcely recognizable by this grandson, who knew it as a boy when it was so run-down.

The fountain which gave the home its name is no more. The big round basin has been filled with soil and shrubs grow where sparkling waters once played. The driveway with its gate and the rustic fence that enclosed the property are gone and the cypress trees that obscured the residence from the street have been cut down. After all, one must expect some changes in seventy years.

There are no young children in the family that occupies the home today, but each Christmas Eve, if the moon is bright, I am told that one can see a miniature sleigh and eight tiny reindeer on the roof of Villa Fontana as Santa Claus stops by to honor an old friend.

Acknowledgments

The few known existing copies of the original edition of Thomas Nast's *Christmas Drawings for the Human Race* are old and worn. Accordingly, if future generations are to enjoy these delightful pictures, a republication was necessary. At the same time it was felt that the addition of some little-known facts about the artist's life would add to the reader's interest. Thus, the original edition, which consisted entirely of drawings, has been augmented by an Introduction and Epilogue. As for the Epilogue, no one living today was privileged to know Thomas Nast as I knew him. Therefore, if this grandson's reminiscences were to be told, this was the time to tell them.

While the republication of a book of drawings might seem a relatively simple undertaking, the incorporation of additional pertinent material, which it is hoped will add to the enjoyment of the drawings, required considerable research. To those who cooperated in making this material available I wish to express my appreciation.

If there was any one spark that ignited the idea for the republication of these drawings it was probably a Christmas card received from the late Raymond Eisenhardt, then president of the engineering-research firm that bears his name. Ray Eisenhardt was, like my grandfather, a man to whom Christmas was a pure delight. The Christmas card referred to was Ray's beautifully written account of the origin of Clement Moore's "Visit from St. Nicholas" upon which I have very briefly drawn.

And this might have been a private printing for the benefit of our children and grandchildren had it not been for Mrs. Betty Goodman, proprietress of the Gallery Bookshop in Mendocino, California, from whom I sought help regarding sources of Santa Claus and Mother Goose material and a possible printer. It was she who encouraged me to submit the idea to Harper & Row, who, in turn, thought the idea of republication a good one.

My thanks to the New-York Historical Society, the New York Public Library, and the American Antiquarian Society for permission to reproduce the pictures from their collections, and special thanks to Mr. Dillon Ripley, Secretary of the Smithsonian Institution, for supplying a copy of the Institution's self-caricature of Thomas Nast with permission to reproduce it, and to the General Theological Seminary of New York City for permission to reproduce their painting of Clement Clarke Moore.

Thanks also to Dr. and Mrs. Franklin W. Rice, present owners of Villa Fontana, the Nast residence in Morristown, New Jersey, for their courtesy in showing Mrs. St. Hill and me through the refurbished home, to Dr. Daniel P. Moynihan for inviting us to the White House to view the self portrait of Thomas hanging in his office and to Mr. W. Parsons Todd for personally conducting us through his exhibit of Nast memorabilia in Macculloch Hall. To Phil Gould of Mendocino, California, my thanks for performing the difficult task of photographing some of the Nast memorabilia in our collection, including the portrait of Sarah Nast and the drawing of "Ignisfatuus Wall Street," both published for the first time.

And thanks to my cousin William R. Battey, a great-grandson of Thomas Nast, and his wife Adarienne, for supplying me with photographs and items of interest. The photographs of Thomas Nast on pages 3 and 100 and the photograph of the painting of Santa Claus on page 25 are from their collection.

Some of the stories about my grandfather narrated in the Epilogue were told to me by my uncle, the late Cyril Nast.

The letters that Thomas Nast wrote to Sarah Edwards Nast while abroad before their marriage are in the Nast collection at the Henry E. Huntington Library, San Marino, California.

I am indebted to the following for their assistance in putting text and pictures together: My granddaughter Sheri Ley, of Orinda, California, for typing the rough draft, and Mrs. Miriam Vashkulat and Mrs. Jeanne Banghart, both of Mendocino, California, for typing the preliminary and final manuscripts, Mr. Seth Heartfield of Harvey's famous restaurant in Washington, D.C., for permission to reproduce the sketch of my grandfather addressing the Canvas-Back Club dinner at Harvey's.

For facts relating to Christmas customs and Santa Claus I have drawn on Clement A. Miles' *Christmas in Ritual and Tradition* and Reginald Nettel's *Santa Claus*. And for information regarding Mother Goose I have relied on William S. and Ceil Baring-Gould's *The Annotated Mother Goose*.

The colonel's account of his reaction to Thomas Nast's *Christmas Eve* drawing in *Harper's Magazine* 1862 Christmas issue, the letter from Mark Twain to my grandfather, and my grandfather's letters from Ecuador to my grandmother, are all quoted from Albert Bigelow Paine's biography *Th: Nast—His Period and His Pictures* (1904). Paine's book is the only one written about my grandfather following personal interviews with the artist and for that reason it is considered the most reliable source of information available. Other excellent illustrated commentaries on Thomas Nast's work are to be found in Chal Vinson's *Thomas Nast: Political Cartoonist* and Morton Keller's *The Art and Politics of Thomas Nast*.

The reader will recognize the quotations from Dickens' *Christmas Carol*.

My special thanks to Mr. Marion S. Wyeth, Jr., Executive Editor of Harper & Row, for his guidance and invaluable editorial assistance.

And last, but by no means least, thanks to my wife Jean for her always constructive help as well as her patience and understanding during the months that her supposedly retired husband remained tied to his desk, writing, rewriting, and researching, as household chores cried out to be done.